DISCARDED

Pinellas Park Public Library
7770   2nd Street North
Pinellas Park, FL 33781

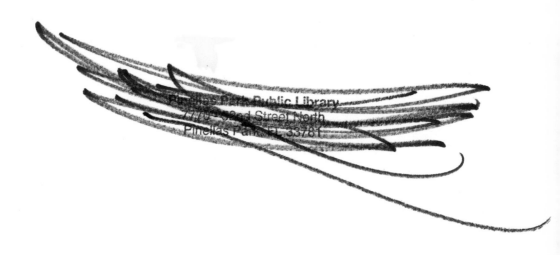

D1064230

Vermont

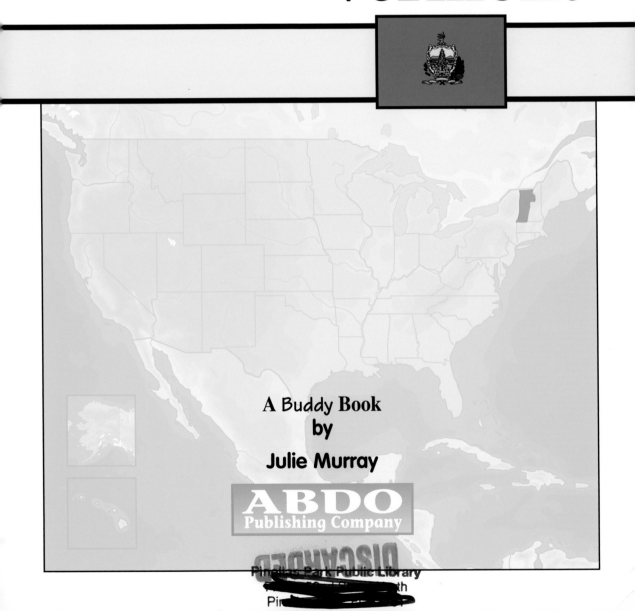

A Buddy Book
by
Julie Murray

ABDO
Publishing Company

DISCARDED

Pinellas Park Public Library

VISIT US AT

www.abdopub.com

Published by ABDO Publishing Company, 4940 Viking Drive, Edina, Minnesota 55435.

Copyright © 2006 by Abdo Consulting Group, Inc. International copyrights reserved in all countries. No part of this book may be reproduced in any form without written permission from the publisher. Buddy Books™ is a trademark and logo of ABDO Publishing Company.

Printed in the United States.

Edited by: Sarah Tieck
Contributing Editor: Michael P. Goecke
Graphic Design: Deb Coldiron, Maria Hosley
Image Research: Sarah Tieck
Photographs: BrandX, Clipart.com, Corbis, Corel, Creatas, Digital Vision, Getty Images, Library of Congress, One Mile Up, Photodisc

Library of Congress Cataloging-in-Publication Data

Murray, Julie, 1969-
   Vermont / Julie Murray.
      p. cm. — (The United States)
   Includes index.
   ISBN 1-59197-704-5
      1. Vermont—Juvenile literature. I. Title.

F49.3.M87 2005
974.3—dc22

                                                    2005048061

Table Of Contents

A Snapshot Of Vermont

When people think of Vermont, they think of its scenic landscape. People also visit to see its red, orange, and yellow tree colors. The trees change colors during the fall months. Vermont is also known for producing maple syrup.

Farms are part of
Vermont's scenic landscape.

There are 50 states in the United States. Every state is different. Every state has an official nickname. Vermont's nickname is the "Green Mountain State." The Green Mountains run through the middle of the state. Even Vermont's name comes from French words meaning "the green mountains."

Farmland in central Vermont.

Vermont became the 14th state on March 4, 1791. It is the seventh-smallest state in the United States. Vermont has 9,615 square miles (24,903 sq km) of land. It is home to 608,827 people. This is the second-smallest state population in the United States. Wyoming is the only state with fewer people.

Where Is Vermont?

There are four parts of the United States. Each part is called a region. Each region is in a different area of the country. The United States Census Bureau says the four regions are the Northeast, the South, the Midwest, and the West.

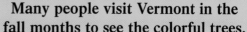

Many people visit Vermont in the fall months to see the colorful trees.

Vermont is located in the Northeast region of the United States. Summers in Vermont are mild with warm temperatures. Winters are snowy and cold. Spring brings rain and thunderstorms. Autumn is one of the favorite times to visit this state. People come to see the vibrant tree colors.

ALASKA

Four Regions of the United States of America

WASHINGTON

MONTANA

NORTH DAKOTA

VERMONT

MAINE

OREGON

MINNESOTA

WISCONSIN

NEW
HAMPSHIRE

MASSACHUSETTS

IDAHO

SOUTH DAKOTA

MICHIGAN

NEW
YORK

RHODE ISLAND
CONNECTICUT

WYOMING

IOWA

PENNSYLVANIA

NEW JERSEY

NEVADA

NEBRASKA

OHIO

DELAWARE

Washington D.C.

UTAH

ILLINOIS

INDIANA

WEST
VIRGINIA

VIRGINIA

MARYLAND

CALIFORNIA

COLORADO

KANSAS

MISSOURI

KENTUCKY

NORTH CAROLINA

ARIZONA

NEW MEXICO

OKLAHOMA

ARKANSAS

TENNESSEE

SOUTH
CAROLINA

MISSISSIPPI

ALABAMA

GEORGIA

TEXAS

LOUISIANA

FLORIDA

HAWAII

	West		Midwest		South		Northeast

Vermont is bordered by three other states and the country of Canada. New Hampshire is east. Massachusetts is south. New York is west. And Canada is north.

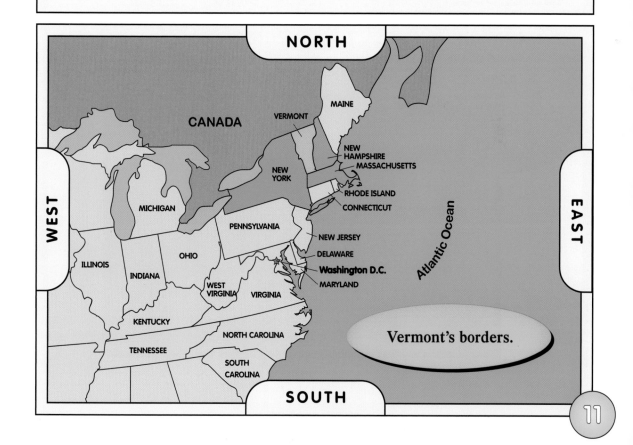

Vermont's borders.

Vermont

State abbreviation: VT

State nickname: Green Mountain State

State capital: Montpelier

State motto: Freedom and Unity

Statehood: March 4, 1791, 14th state

Population: 608,827, ranks 49th

State flag:
Adopted in 1923

Land area: 9,615 square miles (24,903 sq km), ranks 43rd

State tree: Sugar maple

State song: "Hail, Vermont!"

State government: Three branches: legislative, executive, and judicial

Average July temperature: 68°F (20°C)

Average January temperature: 17°F (-8°C)

State bird:
Hermit thrush

State animal:
Morgan horse

State flower:
Red clover

Cities And The Capital

The capital city of Vermont is Montpelier. It is located in the middle of the state. Montpelier has 8,035 residents. Its population is the smallest of all the state capital cities in the United States.

Burlington is Vermont's largest city. It is located on Lake Champlain in northwestern Vermont. Burlington is home to the University of Vermont. Burlington is where Ben and Jerry's Homemade Ice Cream was first created in 1978.

Vermont's State Capitol

Famous Citizens

Calvin Coolidge (1872–1933)

Calvin Coolidge was born in Plymouth Notch in 1872. He was the 30th president of the United States. Before that, he was vice president of the United States under President Warren G. Harding. When Harding died in 1923, Coolidge became the president. He was elected in 1924 for a four-year term. Some people called him "Silent Cal."

Calvin Coolidge

Famous Citizens

Patty Sheehan (1956–)

Patty Sheehan was born in Middlebury in 1956. She is famous for being a professional golfer. She has received many awards for playing golf. She has had more than 30 victories in her career. She was inducted into the Ladies Professional Golf Association Hall of Fame in 1993.

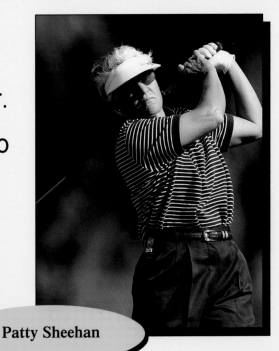

Patty Sheehan

Maple Syrup

The sugar maple is the state tree of Vermont. It is a very important tree in this state. That is because Vermont is a leading producer of maple syrup in the United States.

A sugar maple tree
in autumn.

The sugar maple produces sap. Sap is
a sugary liquid that comes out of the tree.
It is used to make maple syrup.

Pinellas Park Public Library
7770 - 52nd Street North
Pinellas Park, FL 33781

Sap is collected in the spring months. To do this, syrup producers use a couple of methods. The old-fashioned way is for people to drill small holes into the bark of the tree. Then, they hang a bucket on the tree. This collects the sap that runs out of the hole. Later, this is boiled to make maple syrup. People usually boil sap in a building called a sugarhouse. It takes more than 30 gallons (114 L) of sap to produce one gallon (four L) of maple syrup.

Lake Champlain

A view of Lake Champlain.

Lake Champlain is the largest lake in Vermont. It is also the sixth-largest freshwater lake in the United States. It has about 490 square miles (1,269 sq km) of area. Its shape is narrow and long.

Lake Champlain is full of
activity throughout the year.

Lake Champlain was named after Samuel de Champlain. It is located on the border between Vermont and New York. The lake's northern tip touches Canada.

People bike and hike on trails around Lake Champlain. They also fish and boat on the lake. During the winter months, people ice skate and ice fish there.

The Green Mountains

Vermont is famous for the Green Mountains. Vermont's highest point, Mount Mansfield, is located there. It stands 4,393 feet (1,339 m) tall. Also, much of the state's granite and marble is mined in the Green Mountains.

Sometimes, it snows in the Green Mountains in the winter months.

The Green Mountains are part of the Appalachian Mountains. The Appalachian Mountains are the second-largest mountain range in North America. They stretch for about 1,500 miles (2,400 km) from Quebec, Canada, to Birmingham, Alabama. The only mountain range in North America that is larger is the Rocky Mountains.

Green Mountain National Forest is found in southern and central Vermont. This area has almost 400,000 acres (161,874 ha) of land. People hike, bike, ski, camp, and fish in Green Mountain National Forest.

Many people visit the Green Mountains in the fall to see the scenery.

Vermont

1609: French explorer Samuel de Champlain explores Vermont.

1666: The French build a fort on Isle La Motte in Lake Champlain.

1724: Fort Drummer is established. This is the first permanent European settlement in Vermont.

1770: Ethan Allen and the Green Mountain Boys start defending Vermont's land from New York settlers.

1775: The Green Mountain Boys take Fort Ticonderoga.

1791: Vermont becomes the 14th state on March 4.

1805: Montpelier becomes the state capital.

1823: Champlain Canal opens. This connects Lake Champlain and the Hudson River in New York.

1881: Chester A. Arthur of Fairfield becomes the 21st president of the United States.

Chester A. Arthur

1923: Calvin Coolidge of Plymouth Notch becomes the 30th president of the United States.

1970: Vermont passes the Environmental Control Law. This protects the environment.

1991: Vermont celebrates its bicentennial.

2005: St. Albans celebrates the 39th Annual Maple Festival.

Cities In Vermont

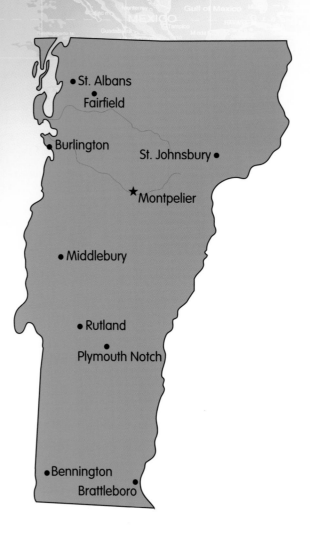

St. Albans
Fairfield
Burlington
St. Johnsbury
★ Montpelier
Middlebury
Rutland
Plymouth Notch
Bennington
Brattleboro

Important Words

bicentennial 200-year anniversary.

capital a city where government leaders meet.

nickname a name that describes something special about a person or a place.

Web Sites

To learn more about Vermont, visit ABDO Publishing Company on the World Wide Web. Web site links about Vermont are featured on our Book Links page. These links are routinely monitored and updated to provide the most current information available.

www.abdopub.com

31

Index

PINELLAS PARK PUBLIC LIBRARY

3 2259 00258 1811

FEB '08

DISCARDED